# CONTENTS 3C

| UNIT 1 | 2 | Where Are You Going? |
|---|---|---|
| UNIT 2 | 10 | Is He Crying? |
| Review 1 | 18 | |
| UNIT 3 | 20 | Can I Have Some Water, Please? |
| UNIT 4 | 28 | What Does He Do? |
| Review 2 | 36 | |
| UNIT 5 | 38 | Do You Exercise Every Day? |
| UNIT 6 | 46 | He Wants a Skateboard |
| Review 3 | 54 | |
| UNIT 7 | 56 | Does She Like Salad? |
| UNIT 8 | 64 | Let's Meet at the Park |
| Review 4 | 72 | |

| Songs | 74 |
|---|---|
| Phonics | 76 |
| Word List | 84 |
| Syllabus | 86 |

# UNIT 1 Where Are You Going?

## Mini Talk Look and listen. 03

Where are you going?

Let's go together.

Bookstore

I'm going to the bookstore.

Okay.

04 CHECK 1 a ☐ b ☐ 2 a ☐ b ☐

# Practice

**A** Listen and write the letter. 05    **B** Listen and repeat. 06

| Where are you going? | I'm going to the park. |

1 park

2 hospital

3 bank

4 bakery

5 toy shop

6 supermarket

7 bookstore

8 zoo

# Listen & Talk

## A Listen and match. 🎧 07

1  2  3  4  5  6

a  b  c  d  e  f

## B Write and say.

> He's/She's going to the ....

1

p_____

2

z_____

3

b_____

# Write & Talk

## A Listen, write, and read. 🎧 08

| to | going | Where |
|----|-------|-------|
| bad | great | hospital |

😊 Hi, Ted. How are you?

😊 I'm _____.

😊 _____ are you going?

😊 I'm going _____ school.

😊 Where is she _____?

😊 She's going to the _____.

She's sick.

😊 That's too _____.

bank
bookstore
toy shop

## B Stick and write. Then ask and answer.

1 A: Where are you going?      B: I'm going to the _____.

2 A: Where is he going?        B: He's going _____.

3 A: Where is she going?       B: She's going _____.

# Story

**Ⓐ Listen, write, and read.** ▶ 🎧09

Where     go     bakery     park     to     going

## B Look and write.

1

I'm going to the _____.

2

We're going to the _____.

3

We're going to the _____.

**Challenge**

Follow, circle, and write.

Where are you going?

I'm going to the _____.

Song 10

## A Listen and number. 🎧11

## B Listen and choose. 🎧12

1

a b

2

a b

3

a b

## C Listen and write T or F. 🎧13

## D Look, check, and write.

**1**

A: Where are _____ going?

B: I'm going to the _____.

☐ park  ☐ bakery

**2**

A: Where is _____ going?

B: She's going to the _____.

☐ bank  ☐ zoo

**3**

A: Where are we _____?

B: We're going to the _____.

☐ toy shop  ☐ bookstore

## E Write and say.

**1** Where are you going?

**2** Where is she going?

## Mini Talk Look and listen. ▶ 🎧16

# Practice

**Ⓐ Listen and write the letter.** 🎧18

**Ⓑ Listen and repeat.** 🎧19

| Is he/she **crying**? | Yes, he/she is. |
| | No, he/she isn't. |

1. crying ☐ — Yes

2. doing homework ☐ — Yes

3. playing tennis ☐ — No

4. playing games ☐ — No

5. riding a bike ☐ — Yes

6. taking a shower ☐ — No

7. driving ☐ — Yes

8. writing an email ☐ — No

# Listen & Talk

## A Listen and choose. 🎧20

**1**
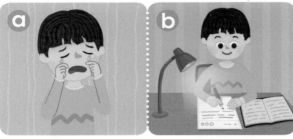

**2**

**3**

**4**

**5**

**6**

## B Write and say.

I'm/He's/She's ....

**1**  I

p_____ tennis

**2**  He

d_____ homework

**3**  She

r_____ a bike

# Write & Talk

## A) Listen, write, and read. 🎧 21

| doing | Where | sleeping |
|---|---|---|
| washing | What | Yes, I am. |

👧 Is Tom _____ homework?

👦 No, he isn't.

👧 _____ is he doing?

👦 He's _____.

👧 _____ are you, Jack?

👦 I'm in the bathroom.

👧 Are you _____ your hands?

👦 _____

## B) Look and write. Then ask and answer.

1  A: Is she _____?

   B: Yes, _____.

2  A: Is she _____?

   B: Yes, _____.

3  A: Is he playing baseball?

   B: _____

   He's _____.

# Story

**A** Listen, write, and read. ▶ 🎧 22

1. Are they _____?
   Yes, they are.

2. Is he _____?
   Yes, he is.

3. Is she playing baseball?
   No, she _____.
   She's _____.

4. I'm scared. Don't come here.

5. Are you okay?
   No, I'm _____.

6. Are you _____? Yes, I am.

| isn't | driving | not | crying | playing tennis | playing games |

## B Read and check.

**1**
A: Is he driving?

B: ☐ Yes, he is.    ☐ No, he isn't.

**2**
A: Is she playing baseball?

B: ☐ Yes, she is.    ☐ No, she isn't.

**3**
A: Is she crying?

B: ☐ Yes, she is.    ☐ No, she isn't.

## Challenge

**Look and write.**

**1**

A: Is he _____?

B: Yes, he is.

**2**

A: Is she doing homework?

B: No, she isn't.

She's _____.

23 Song

# Check-Up

## A Listen and write T or F. 24

**1**

**2**

**3**

## B Listen and choose. 25

**1**
ⓐ ⓑ

**2**
ⓐ ⓑ

**3**
ⓐ ⓑ

## C Listen and match. 26

**1**

**2**

**3**

**4**

ⓐ

ⓑ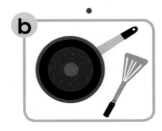

ⓒ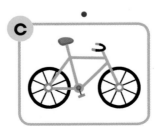

ⓓ

## D Look, check, and write.

**1**

A: Is she _____?

☐ crying  ☐ driving

B: Yes, she is.

**2**

A: Is he playing basketball?

B: No, he isn't. He's _____.

☐ playing tennis  ☐ writing an email

**3**

A: Are you _____?

☐ playing games  ☐ doing homework

B: Yes, _____.

## E Write and say.

**1**

Yes, she is.

**2**

Are you washing your hands?

No, I'm not.

_____

# Review ①

## Ⓐ Look and write.

1     book____ ____ore

2     su____er____arket

3     ____ospi____al

4     b____n____

5     b____ke____y

6     p____ ____k

7     d____i____ing

8     ____r____ing

9     pla____ing ____ennis

10     ri____ing a bi____e

**B** **Look and write.**

Where are you going?

1   I'm going to the _____.

2   _____

3   _____

4   _____

| bookstore | zoo | hospital | toy shop |

**C** **Read and write T or F.**

1
A: Is he washing the dishes?
B: Yes, he is. ☐

2
A: Is she doing homework?
B: Yes, she is. ☐

3
A: Is he cooking?
B: No, he isn't.
   He's playing games. ☐

4
A: Is she writing an email?
B: No, she isn't.
   She's riding a bike. ☐

# Can I Have Some Water, Please?

**Mini Talk** Look and listen. ▶ 🎧29

# Practice

**A** Listen and write the letter. 🎧31  **B** Listen and repeat. 🎧32

> Can I have some **tea**, please? | Sure. Here you are.

tea ☐ ①

soup ☐ ②

lemonade ☐ ③

iced water ☐ ④

chips ⑤ ☐

hot dogs ☐ ⑥

cereal ☐ ⑦

# Listen & Talk

**A** Listen and match. 🎧 33

1

2

3

4

5

6

**B** Write and say.

> Can I have some ..., please?

1

t_____

2

l_____

3

h_____

# Write & Talk

**(A) Listen, write, and read.** 🎧 34

| some | have | Sure. |
| hungry | tea | Can |

I'm _____. _____ I

have some apple pie, please?

Sure. Have _____ milk, too.

Thank you.

Do you want some _____?

No, thanks. Can I _____

some water, please?

_____ Here you are.

**(B) Look and write. Then say.**

pizza    hot dogs    lemonade    chips

1  Have some _____.

3  Have some _____.

2  Have some _____.

4  Have some _____.

# Story

**A** Listen, write, and read. ▶ 🎧35

1. No more ice cream!
   Okay.

2. Can I have some _____, please?
   Sure.

3. Hiccup!

4. Can I have _____ water, please?
   Hiccup!
   Sure. Here _____ are.

5. Have some _____.
   Hiccup!

6. Can I _____ some ice cream, please?
   Sure. Here you are.

7. No more hiccups!

| some | you | lemonade | have | hot dogs |

**B** **Read and number in order. Then match.**

( ) Can I have some water, please? •

( ) Can I have some ice cream, please? •

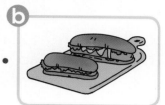

( ) Can I have some hot dogs, please? •

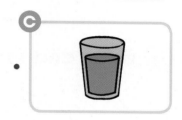

**Choose and write.**

A: I'm _____.

Can I have some _____, please?

B: Sure. Here you are.

# Check-Up

**A** Listen and number. 🎧 37

**B** Listen and write T or F. 🎧 38

1

2

3

**C** Listen, choose, and match. 🎧 39

| 1 | thirsty | cold | | 2 | hungry | cold | | 3 | thirsty | hungry |

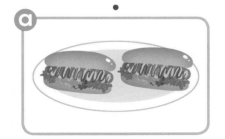

## D Look, check, and write.

**1**

I'm _____.

☐ thirsty   ☐ cold

Can I have some water, please?

**2**

A: Have _____.

☐ some soup   ☐ some chips

B: Thank you.

**3**

A: Can I have _____, please?

☐ some tea   ☐ some hot dogs

B: Sure. Here you are.

## E Write and say.

**1** [ _____ ]

Sure. Here you are.

**2** [ _____ ]

Sure. Here you are.

# What Does He Do?

## Mini Talk Look and listen.

# Practice

**A** Listen and write the letter. 🎧 44    **B** Listen and repeat. 🎧 45

What does he/she do?    He's/She's a scientist.

scientist ☐

dancer ☐

vet ☐

dentist ☐

model ☐

soccer player ☐

bus driver ☐

farmer ☐

# Listen & Talk

## Ⓐ Listen and mark O or X. 🎧46

1

2

3

4

5

6

## Ⓑ Write and say.

He's/She's/They're ....

1 He

a v_____

2 She

a b_____

3 They

s_____s

# Write & Talk

## A Listen, write, and read. 🎧47

| mom | do | soccer player |
|-----|-----|---------------|
| uncle | she | police officer |

Who is he?

He's my _____.

What does he _____?

He's a _____.

That's my _____.

Is _____ a singer?

No, she isn't. She's a _____.

Great!

## B Match and write. Then ask and answer.

| dentists firefighter cook |
|---|

 1    2    3

a          b          c

1   What does she do?

She's a _____.

2   What does he do?

He's a _____.

3   What do they do?

They're _____.

# Story

**A** Listen, write, and read. ▶ 🎧 48

1. What does she _____?
   She's a _____.

2. Wow! She's _____.

3. Are they _____?
   No, they _____.
   They're dancers.

4. What _____ he do?
   He's a singer.

6. I love him.

singers    tall    does    model    do    aren't

## B Read, match, and check.

1

What does she do? •

• ☐ Yes, they are.
☐ No, they aren't.

2

Are they singers? •

• ☐ He's a dancer.
☐ He's a singer.

3

What does he do? •

• ☐ She's a model.
☐ She's a cook.

## Challenge

**Stick, choose, and write.**

Sticker  Sticker  Sticker  Sticker

He's a _____ . She's a _____ .

49 Song

# Check-Up

## A Listen and choose. 50

**1**
ⓐ ⓑ

**2**
ⓐ ⓑ

**3**
ⓐ ⓑ

## B Listen and match. 51

**1**  •

**2**  •

**3**  •

**4**  •

ⓐ

ⓑ

ⓒ

ⓓ

## C Listen and write T or F. 52

**1**

**2**

**3**

## D Look, check, and write.

**1**

This is my grandpa.

He's a _____.

☐ dentist    ☐ farmer

**2**

A: What does _____ do?

B: She's a _____.

☐ vet    ☐ singer

**3**

A: Is he a _____?

☐ dancer    ☐ scientist

B: Yes, _____ is.

## E Write and say.

**1** What does she do?

**2** What does he do?

**A** **Look and number.**

- ◯ chips
- ◯ tea
- ◯ lemonade
- ◯ hot dogs

- ◯ thirsty
- ◯ hungry
- ◯ cold

- ◯ vet
- ◯ dancer
- ◯ soccer player
- ◯ bus driver

**B** **Read and match.**

1 I'm hungry.

2 I'm thirsty.

3 I'm cold.

Can I have some cereal, please?

Can I have some iced water, please?

Can I have some soup, please?

**C** **Look and write.**

a farmer   a model   a dentist   a scientist

1 A: What does he do?

B: _____

2 A: What does she do?

B: _____

3 A: What does he do?

B: _____

4 A: What does she do?

B: _____

# Do You Exercise Every Day?

## Mini Talk Look and listen. ▶ 🎧 55

Do you exercise every day?

Okay.

Yes, I do.
Let's jump rope together.

# Practice

**A** Listen and write the letter. 🎧57    **B** Listen and repeat. 🎧58

Do you get up early every day?   Yes, I do.
                                  No, I don't.

# Listen & Talk

## (A) Listen, number, and circle. 🎧59

Yes No

Yes No

Yes No

Yes No

Yes No

Yes No

## (B) Write and say

I ... every day.

**1**

d_____ soda

**2**

w_____ a diary

**3**

c_____ my room

# Write & Talk

## A Listen, write, and read. 🎧 60

| do | write | soda |
|----|-------|------|
| not | drink | diary |

What's that?

It's my _____.

Do you _____ a diary every day?

Yes, I _____.

Do you like _____?

Yes, I do.

I _____ soda every day.

Oh, no! That's _____ good.

## B Look and write. Then ask and answer.

take a bath     read a book
clean your room

1  A: Do you _____ every day?     B: _____, _____.

2  A: Do you _____ every day?     B: _____, _____.

3  A: Do you _____ every day?     B: _____, _____.

# Story

**A** Listen, write, and read. ▶ 61

drink soda    exercise    fly    do    watch TV    don't

## B Read and check.

**1**

A: Do you watch TV every day?

B: ☐ Yes, I do.  ☐ No, I don't.

**2**

A: Do you drink soda every day?

B: ☐ Yes, I do.  ☐ No, I don't.

**3**

A: Do you exercise every day?

B: ☐ Yes, I do.  ☐ No, I don't.

## Challenge

### What do you do every day? Check and write.

I _____ every day.

# Check-Up

## A Listen and choose. 🎧 63

**1**

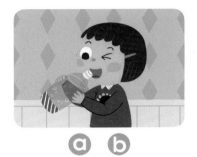

ⓐ ⓑ

**2**

ⓐ ⓑ

**3**

ⓐ ⓑ

## B Listen, choose, and circle. 🎧 64

**1** ⓐ ⓑ

Yes No

**2** ⓐ ⓑ

Yes No

**3** ⓐ ⓑ

Yes No

## C Listen, number, and match. 🎧 65

Yes, I do.

No, I don't.

## D Look, check, and write.

**1**

A: Do you _____ every day?

☐ get up early    ☐ eat breakfast

B: No, I don't.

**2**

A: Do you _____ every day?

☐ drink milk    ☐ eat ice cream

B: Yes, I do.

**3**

A: Do you _____ every day?

☐ take a bath    ☐ write a diary

B: _____

## E Write and say.

**1**

Yes, I do.

**2**

No, I don't.

## Mini Talk Look and listen. ▶ 🎧 68

# Practice

**A** Listen and write the letter. 🎧70    **B** Listen and repeat. 🎧71

What does he/she want?    He/She wants a drone.

1. a drone ☐
2. a skateboard ☐
3. a tennis racket ☐
4. a swim tube ☐
5. a computer ☐
6. a game player ☐
7. in-line skates ☐
8. soccer shoes ☐

# Listen & Talk

**A** Listen and stick. 🎧72

**B** Write and say.

He/She wants ....

1    a d_____

2    a s_____

3    s_____

# Write & Talk

## A Listen, write, and read. 🎧 73

| | |
|---|---|
| want | does | swim tube |
| Do | doesn't | tennis racket |

Ken _____ want in-line skates.

What does he _____?

He wants a _____.

He likes tennis.

_____ you want a beach ball?

Yes, I do.

What _____ she want?

She wants a _____.

## B Look and write. Then say.

| | |
|---|---|
| shoes | a backpack |
| a bike | a skateboard |

**1**

He wants _____.

He doesn't want _____.

**2**

She wants _____.

She doesn't want _____.

# Story

**A** Listen, write, and read.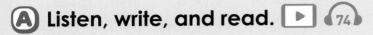

1. What _____ you want, Jane?
   I want _____ .

2. What _____ Jack want?
   He _____ a game player.

3. What does Emily want?
   _____ wants a hair band.

4. Thanks, Dad.

5. I want a game player.
   I want a hair band, _____ .

6. It's mine.

does    She    too    a drone    do    wants

50

## B Write and match.

1  Jane wants _____. •

2  Jack wants _____. •

3 Emily wants _____. •

a

b

c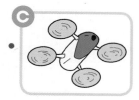

## Challenge

**Circle and write.**

1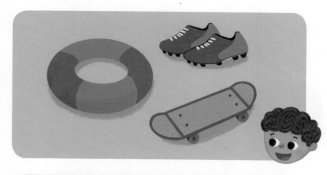

A: What does he want?

B: He _____.

2

A: What does she want?

B: She _____.

75 Song

# Check-Up

## A Listen and number. 76

## B Listen and choose. 77

1    a  b

2    a  b

3    a  b

## C Listen and match. 78

1   2   3

a    b    c    d

## D Look, check, and write.

**1**

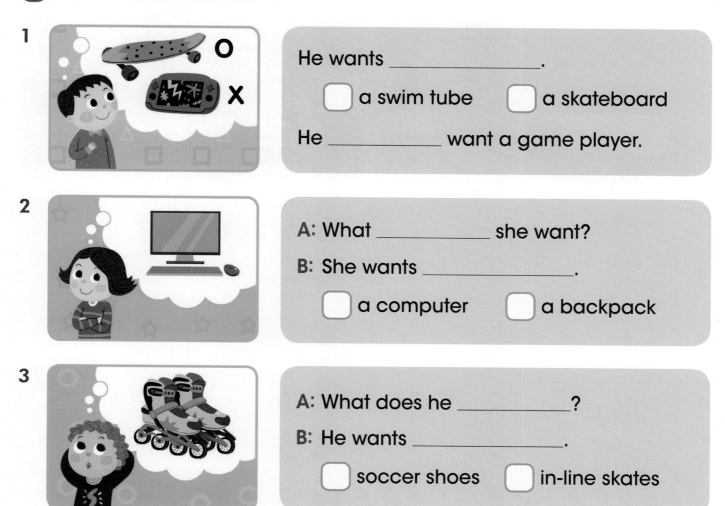

He wants _____.

☐ a swim tube     ☐ a skateboard

He _____ want a game player.

**2**

A: What _____ she want?

B: She wants _____.

☐ a computer     ☐ a backpack

**3**

A: What does he _____?

B: He wants _____.

☐ soccer shoes     ☐ in-line skates

## E Write and say.

**1**

What does he want?

**2**

What does she want?

# Review 3

**A** Look, match, and write.

| | | | | |
|---|---|---|---|---|
| 1 | take | • | • your room | _____ |
| 2 | clean | • | • breakfast | _____ |
| 3 | write | • | • a diary | _____ |
| 4 | eat | • | • a bath | _____ |
| 5 | a game | • | • shoes | _____ |
| 6 | soccer | • | • tube | _____ |
| 7 | a swim | • | • player | _____ |
| 8 | a tennis | • | • racket | _____ |

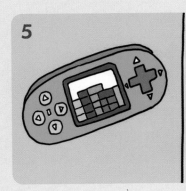

**B** **Look and write.**

1 **A:** Do you exercise every day? **B:** _____ , _____ .

2 **A:** Do you drink soda every day? **B:** _____ , _____ .

3 **A:** Do you eat breakfast every day? **B:** _____ , _____ .

4 **A:** Do you get up early every day? **B:** _____ , _____ .

**C** **Look and write**

What does he/she want?

1 _____

2 _____

3 _____

4 _____

a drone
a skateboard
a computer
in-line skates

# Does She Like Salad?

## Mini Talk Look and listen. ▶ 🎧81

# Practice

**A** Listen and write the letter. 🎧 83

**B** Listen and repeat. 🎧 84

| Does he/she like fruit? | Yes, he/she does. |
| | No, he/she doesn't. |

fruit ☐  curry ☐  steak ☐  spaghetti ☐

vegetables ☐  sandwiches ☐  hamburgers ☐  dumplings ☐

# Listen & Talk

**A** Listen, number, and circle. 🎧 85

**B** Write and say.

> He/She likes ....
> He/She doesn't like ....

1    s_____

2    h_____

3    v_____

58

# Write & Talk

## A Listen, write, and read. 🎧 86

| she | doesn't | likes |
|-----|---------|-------|
| fruit | making | like |

👧 Does Ben _____ hamburgers?

👦 No, he _____ .

👦 What does he like?

👦 He _____ chicken.

👦 I'm _____ fruit juice.

It's for my mom·

👧 Does your mom like _____ ?

👦 Yes, _____ does.

## B Look and write. Then say.

| fish | cake |
|------|------|
| curry | spaghetti |

1 He likes _____ .

2 He doesn't like _____ .

3 She _____ .

4 She _____ .

# Story

**A** Listen, write, and read. ▶ 🎧87

**1** Does she like milk?

No, she _____.

**2** Does she like _____?

No, she doesn't.

**3** What does she like?

She _____ fruit.

**4** Do you _____ fruit?

Yes, I do.

**5** This is for you.

I like _____, but I _____ like apples.

**6**

| likes | vegetables | don't | fruit | like | doesn't |

## B Read and check.

**1**
- [ ] She likes milk.
- [ ] She doesn't like milk.

**2**
- [ ] She likes vegetables.
- [ ] She doesn't like vegetables.

**3**
- [ ] I don't like apples.
- [ ] I don't like fruit.

## Challenge

**Stick and write.**

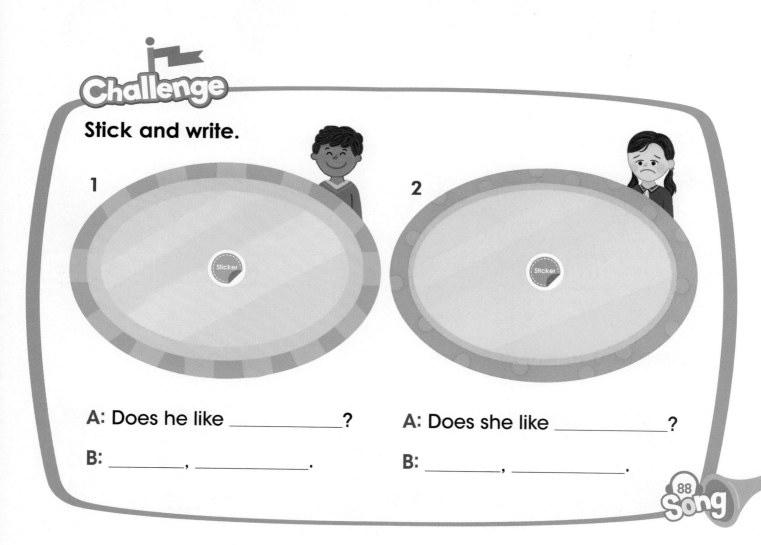

**1**

A: Does he like _____?

B: _____, _____.

**2**

A: Does she like _____?

B: _____, _____.

# Check-Up

**A** Listen and choose. 🎧89

1

2

3

**B** Listen, match, and circle. 🎧90

1

2

3

4

a Yes No

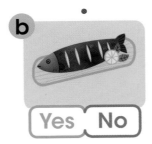
b Yes No

c Yes No

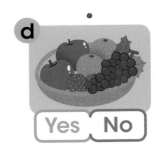
d Yes No

**C** Listen and write T or F. 🎧91

1

2

3

# D Look, check, and write.

**1**

He likes _____.

☐ steak      ☐ pizza

He _____ like curry.

**2**

A: Does she like _____?

☐ vegetables      ☐ fruit

B: _____

**3**

A: Does he like _____?

☐ hamburgers      ☐ sandwiches

B: _____

# E Write and say.

**1**

Yes, he does.

**2**

Does she like dumplings?

# Let's Meet at the Park

## Mini Talk Look and listen. ▶ 🎧94

Let's play basketball, Ben.

Sounds good.

Let's meet at the park. How about at 4 o'clock?

Okay. See you.

🎧95 CHECK  1 a ☐ b ☐  2 a ☐ b ☐

# Practice

**A** Listen and write the letter. 🎧96    **B** Listen and repeat. 🎧97

Let's meet at the mall.
How about at 1 o'clock?

Okay. See you.

1 mall

2 playground

3 library

4 museum

5 bus stop

6 swimming pool

7 subway station

# Listen & Talk

## A Listen, number, and write the time. 🎧 98

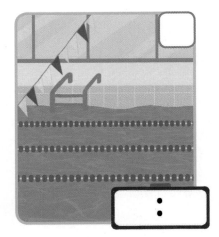

## B Write and say.

> Let's meet at the ... at ....

**1**

m_____

**2**

p_____

**3**

s_____

# Write & Talk

**Ⓐ Listen, write, and read.** 🎧 99

| in | mall | See you. |
|---|---|---|
| at | exercise | How about |

🧒 Let's _____ together.

🧒 Sounds good.

🧒 Let's meet _____ the gym.

🧒 Okay. _____

🧒 Let's meet at the _____ at 10.

🧒 Sorry. I'm busy _____ the

morning. _____ at 2?

🧒 Okay.

**Ⓑ Look and write. Then ask and answer.**

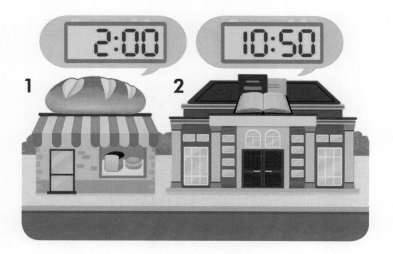

| bakery | hospital |
|---|---|
| playground | library |

**1** A: Let's meet at the _____.

How about at _____?

B: Okay. See you.

**2** A: Let's meet at the _____.

How about at _____?

B: Okay. See you.

# Story

**Ⓐ Listen, write, and read.** ▶ 🎧100

1. Let's go to the _____ today.
   Sorry, I can't. I'm busy today.

2. _____ Sunday?
   Sounds good.

3. Let's _____ at the subway station.
   Okay. How about at 1 o'clock?

4. It's too _____.

5. How about _____ 11 o'clock?
   Okay.
   _____

6.

---

How about     meet     at     late     See you.     museum

**B** Look and circle.

1

Let's go to the ( museum / library ).

2

Let's meet at the ( bus stop / subway station ).

3

How about at ( one / eleven ) o'clock?

Challenge

Choose, draw, and write.

Let's meet at the _____.

How about at _____?

# Check-Up

## A Listen and choose. 🎧102

**1**

(a) (b)

**2**

(a) (b)

**3**

(a) (b)

## B Listen, number, and match. 🎧103

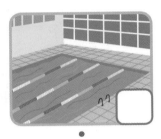

## C Listen and choose. 🎧104

**1**

(a) (b)

**2**
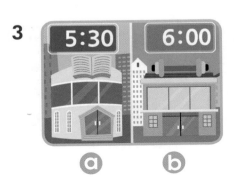
(a) (b)

**3**
(a) (b)

## D  Look, write, and circle.

**1**

A: Let's meet at the _____ .

How about ( at three / at seven ) o'clock?

B: Okay.

**2**

A: Let's meet at the _____ .

How about ( at six fifty / at eight thirty )?

B: Okay.

**3**

A: Let's meet at the _____

( at nine forty / at ten twenty ).

B: Okay. See you.

## E  Write and say.

**1**

Let's meet _____ .
How about _____ ?

Okay.

**2**

Let's meet at the _____
at _____ .

Okay.

## A  Look, circle, and write.

1 _____
hamburgers / curry

2 _____
dumplings / chicken

3 _____
vegetables / fruit

4 _____
salad / spaghetti

5 _____
steak / sandwiches

6 _____
museum / playground

7 _____
gym / mall

8 _____
swimming pool / hospital

9 _____
subway station / bus stop

10 _____
library / bakery

## Ⓑ Read and match.

1   Does she like vegetables?   •        • ⓐ Yes, she does.

2   Does he like sandwiches?   •        • ⓑ No, she doesn't.

3   Does she like hamburgers?   •        • ⓒ No, he doesn't.

## Ⓒ Write and circle.

1   A: Let's meet _____.
    How about at ( four o'clock / four ten )?
    B: Okay. See you.

2   A: Let's meet _____.
    How about at ( six fifty / six fifteen )?
    B: Okay. See you.

3   A: Let's meet _____.
    How about at ( two thirty / three twenty )?
    B: Okay. See you.

| at the gym | at the subway station | at the museum |

# Songs

## Unit 1 Where Are You Going? 🎧10

Where, where are you going?

I'm going to the park, park.

I'm going to the bank, bank.

Where, where are you going?

I'm going to the bakery, bakery.

I'm going to the hospital, hospital.

## Unit 2 Is He Crying? 🎧23

Is he crying?

Yes, he is. He's crying.

Is she doing homework?

Yes, she is. She's doing homework.

Is he playing tennis?

No, he isn't. He's riding a bike.

## Unit 3 Can I Have Some Tea, Please? 🎧36

I'm cold. I'm cold.

Can I have some tea, please?

Sure. Here you are.

Oh, thank you.

I'm hungry. I'm hungry.

Can I have some chips, please?

Sure. Here you are.

Oh, thank you.

## Unit 4 What Does He do? 🎧49

What does he do? What does he do?

He's a farmer.

He's a dentist. *Great!*

What does she do? What does she do?

She's a model.

She's a scientist. *Wow!*

## Unit 5 Do You Get Up Early Every Day? 🎧62

Do you get up early every day?

Yes, yes. Yes, I do.

Do you eat breakfast every day?

No, no. No, I don't.

Do you drink soda every day?

Yes, yes. Yes, I do.

Do you exercise every day?

No, no. No, I don't.

## Unit 6 He Wants a Drone 🎧75

What does he want?

He wants a drone.

He wants a tennis racket.

What does she want?

She wants a skateboard.

She wants soccer shoes.

## Unit 7 Does He Like Vegetables? 🎧88

Oh, vegetables!

Does he like vegetables?

Yes, he does.

He likes vegetables.

Oh, fruit!

Does she like fruit?

No, she doesn't.

She doesn't like fruit.

## Unit 8 Let's Meet at the Library 🎧101

Let's meet at the library.

How about at one o'clock?

Okay. Okay. See you.

Let's meet at the museum.

How about at two thirty?

Okay. Okay. See you.

# Phonics ①

## Ⓐ Listen and repeat. Then read. 🎧105

au
aw

1 au → August

2 au → autumn

3 au → sauce

4 aw → saw

5 aw → draw

6 aw → straw

## Ⓑ Listen and check. 🎧106

1
☐ sauce
☐ saw

2
☐ August
☐ draw

3
☐ straw
☐ sauce

4
☐ draw
☐ autumn

## Ⓒ Circle and match.

1

au | aw
•

•
saw

2
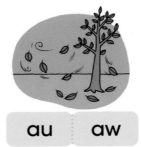

au | aw
•

•
straw

3

au | aw
•

•
autumn

# Phonics ②

## (A) Listen and repeat. Then read. 🎧107

oi
oy

1 oi → coin

2 oi → boil

3 oi → toilet

4 oy → boy

5 oy → toy

6 oy → joy

## (B) Listen and circle. 🎧108

1
boy
boil

2
toy
toilet

3
coin
toy

4
boil
joy

## (C) Match and write.

1 •

2 •

3 •

• c___ ___n

• b___ ___

• t___ ___let

**A** Listen and repeat. Then read. 🎧109

**ou**
**ow**

1 ou → mouse

2 ou → cloud

3 ou → count

4 ow → cow

5 ow → down

6 ow → brown

**B** Listen and check. 🎧110

1  ☐ cloud
   ☐ down

2  ☐ mouse
   ☐ brown

3  ☐ mouse
   ☐ cloud

4  ☐ count
   ☐ down

**C** Circle and write.

1

| ou | ow |

c___ ___

2

| ou | ow |

c___ ___nt

3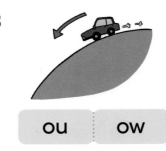

| ou | ow |

d___ ___n

**Ⓐ Listen, circle, and write.** 🎧111

1  au  oi  ow    2  aw  oy  ou    3  aw  oi  ow    4  au  oy  ou

c___ ___n        str___ ___        d___ ___n        ___ ___tumn

**Ⓑ Listen, circle, and match.** 🎧112

1  boy         2  toy          3  brown        4  August
   boil            toilet          draw            mouse

**Ⓒ Check and write.**

1  ☐ oi    2  ☐ aw    3  ☐ ou
   ☐ au       ☐ ow       ☐ oy

s___ ___ce        dr___ ___        cl___ ___d

# Phonics 5

**A** Listen and repeat. Then read. 113

hard **C**

soft **C**

1  c → **c**olor

2  c → **c**at

3  c → **c**old

4  c → **c**ent

5  c → ri**c**e

6  c → spa**c**e

**B** Listen and check. 114

1  ☐ cent
   ☐ cat

2  ☐ space
   ☐ cold

3  ☐ cold
   ☐ cent

4  ☐ color
   ☐ space

**C** Write and match.

1

c ☐ ☐ ☐

2

☐ ☐ c ☐

3

c ☐ ☐ ☐

 hard c

 soft c

80

## Ⓐ Listen and repeat. Then read. 🎧115

hard **g**

soft **g**

1 g → **g**ame

2 g → **g**o

3 g → **g**ood

4 g → ma**g**ic

5 g → **g**ym

6 g → pa**g**e

## Ⓑ Listen and circle. 🎧116

1 magic
game

2 good
page

3 gym
go

4 gym
good

## Ⓒ Write and match.

1

g ☐ ☐

2

g ☐ ☐ ☐

3

☐ ☐ g ☐

hard g

soft g

# Phonics 7

## A Listen and repeat. Then read. 🎧117

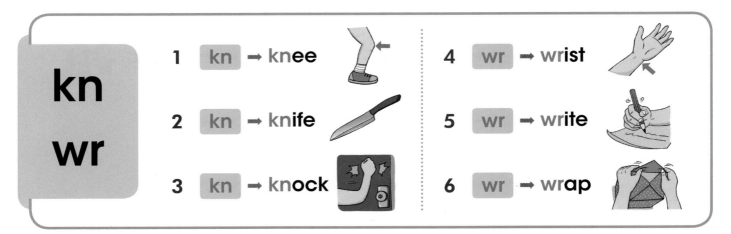

| | | | |
|---|---|---|---|
| 1 | kn → kn**ee** | 4 | wr → wr**ist** |
| 2 | kn → kn**ife** | 5 | wr → wr**ite** |
| 3 | kn → kn**ock** | 6 | wr → wr**ap** |

kn
wr

## B Listen and check. 🎧118

1
- [ ] wrist
- [ ] knee

2
- [ ] wrap
- [ ] knock

3
- [ ] write
- [ ] knock

4
- [ ] write
- [ ] knife

## C Circle and write.

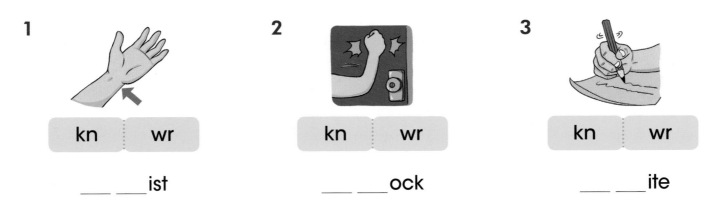

1
kn    wr

___ ___ist

2
kn    wr

___ ___ock

3
kn    wr

___ ___ite

**A** Listen, circle, and write. 🎧119

1 | soft c   soft g

___ent

2 | hard c   hard g

___ood

3 | kn   wr

___ ___ite

4 | kn   wr

___ ___ock

**B** Listen, circle, and match. 🎧120

1 | knock
wrap

2 | go
cold

3 | page
rice

4 | knife
wrist

**C** Check and write.

1 | ☐ c
☐ g

___olor

2 | ☐ c
☐ g

ma___ic

3 | ☐ kn
☐ wr

___ ___ee

# Word List 3C

## Unit 1 — Where Are You Going?

bakery  _____

bank  _____

bookstore  _____

hospital  _____

park  _____

school  _____

sick  _____

supermarket  _____

to  _____

together  _____

toy shop  _____

where  _____

zoo  _____

## Unit 2 — Is He Crying?

cooking  _____

crying  _____

doing homework  _____

driving  _____

playing baseball  _____

playing games  _____

playing tennis  _____

riding a bike  _____

scared  _____

sleeping  _____

taking a shower  _____

washing the dishes  _____

writing an email  _____

## Unit 3 — Can I Have Some Water, Please?

cereal  _____

chips  _____

cold  _____

delicious  _____

hiccups  _____

hot dogs  _____

hungry  _____

iced water  _____

lemonade  _____

some  _____

soup  _____

tea  _____

thirsty  _____

## Unit 4 — What Does He Do?

bus driver  _____

cook  _____

dancer  _____

dentist  _____

doctor  _____

farmer  _____

firefighter  _____

model  _____

police officer  _____

scientist  _____

singer  _____

soccer player  _____

vet  _____

## Unit 5 · Do You Exercise Every Day?

clean your room _____

drink milk _____

drink soda _____

eat breakfast _____

every day _____

exercise _____

get up early _____

hurry up _____

jump rope _____

read a book _____

take a bath _____

watch TV _____

write a diary _____

## Unit 6 · He Wants a Skateboard

a computer _____

a drone _____

a game player _____

a skateboard _____

a swim tube _____

a tennis racket _____

backpack _____

beach ball _____

hair band _____

in-line skates _____

mine _____

soccer shoes _____

want _____

## Unit 7 · Does She Like Salad?

chicken _____

curry _____

dumplings _____

fish _____

fruit _____

hamburgers _____

onions _____

salad _____

sandwiches _____

spaghetti _____

steak _____

strawberries _____

vegetables _____

## Unit 8 · Let's Meet at the Park

at _____

bus stop _____

busy _____

How about ...? _____

in the morning _____

library _____

mall _____

meet _____

museum _____

playground _____

subway station _____

swimming pool _____

too late _____

# Syllabus 3C

## Unit 1  Where Are You Going?

| Structures | Vocabulary | | Phonics |
|---|---|---|---|
| • Where are you going? | park | supermarket | Vowel Digraphs |
| I'm going to the park. | hospital | bookstore | au, aw |
| • Where is he/she going? | bank | zoo | |
| He's/She's going to the bank. | bakery | school | |
| • Let's go together. - Okay. | toy shop | where | |

## Unit 2  Is He Crying?

| Structures | Vocabulary | | Phonics |
|---|---|---|---|
| • Are you cooking? | crying | playing games | Diphthongs |
| Yes, I am. / No, I'm not. | driving | riding a bike | oi, oy |
| • Is he/she crying? | sleeping | taking a shower | |
| Yes, he/she is. / No, he/she isn't. | doing homework | writing an email | |
| • I'm/He's/She's in the kitchen. | playing tennis | washing the dishes | |

**Review 1**

## Unit 3  Can I Have Some Water, Please?

| Structures | Vocabulary | | Phonics |
|---|---|---|---|
| • Can I have some water, please? | tea | cereal | Diphthongs |
| Sure. Here you are. | soup | apple pie | ou, ow |
| • I'm thirsty. | lemonade | ice cream | |
| • Have some milk. | iced water | cold | |
| • Do you want some tea? - No, thanks. | chips | thirsty | |
| • No more ice cream! | hot dogs | hungry | |

## Unit 4  What Does He Do?

| Structures | Vocabulary | | Phonics |
|---|---|---|---|
| • What does he/she do? | scientist | soccer player | Review: |
| He's/She's a vet. | dancer | bus driver | Vowel Digraphs<br>au, aw |
| • Is he/she a farmer? | vet | farmer | Diphthongs |
| Yes, he/she is. / No, he/she isn't. | model | police officer | oi, oy, ou, ow |
| • Who's he? - He's my uncle. | dentist | firefighter | |

**Review 2**

## Unit 5  Do You Exercise Every Day?

| Structures | Vocabulary | | Phonics |
|---|---|---|---|
| • Do you exercise every day? | exercise | write a diary | Hard c, Soft c |
|   Yes, I do. / No, I don't. | get up early | take a bath | |
| • I get up early every day. | eat breakfast | ride a bike | |
| • Do you like soda? - Yes, I do. | drink soda/milk | read a book | |
| • That's not good. | clean my/your room | watch TV | |

## Unit 6  He Wants a Skateboard

| Structures | Vocabulary | | Phonics |
|---|---|---|---|
| • What does he/she want? | a drone | a swim tube | Hard g, Soft g |
|   He/She wants a skateboard. | a computer | a game player | |
| • He/She doesn't want shoes. | a skateboard | a beach ball | |
| • What do you want? | a backpack | in-line skates | |
|   I want a bike. | a tennis racket | soccer shoes | |
| **Review 3** | | | |

## Unit 7  Does She Like Salad?

| Structures | Vocabulary | | Phonics |
|---|---|---|---|
| • Does he/she like salad? | fruit | vegetables | Silent Letters |
|   Yes, he/she does. | curry | sandwiches | kn, wr |
|   No, he/she doesn't. | steak | hamburgers | |
| • What does he/she like? | spaghetti | dumplings | |
|   He/She likes steak. | fish | onions | |

## Unit 8  Let's Meet at the Park

| Structures | Vocabulary | | Phonics |
|---|---|---|---|
| • Let's meet at the mall (at two). - Okay. | mall | swimming pool | Review: |
| • How about at 3 o'clock? | playground | bus stop | Hard/Soft c |
|   Okay. See you. | library | subway station | Hard/Soft g |
| • Let's go to the swimming pool. | museum | bakery | Silent Letters kn, wr |
|   Sounds good. / Sorry, I can't. | gym | hospital | |
| **Review 4** | | | |

## 11 Read and choose.
다음을 읽고 알맞은 그림을 고르세요.

> He's playing games.

ⓐ    ⓑ

ⓒ    ⓓ

## [12-13] Look and choose.
그림을 보고 알맞은 것을 고르세요.

### 12

ⓐ Can I have some salad, please?
ⓑ Can I have some lemonade, please?
ⓒ Can I have some chips, please?
ⓓ Can I have some cereal, please?

### 13

ⓐ He's going to the zoo.
ⓑ He's going to the toy shop.
ⓒ She's going to the bookstore.
ⓓ She's going to the mall.

## 14 Look and write.
그림을 보고 빈칸에 알맞은 단어를 쓰세요.

A: What does she do?
B: She's a _____.

## 15 Unscramble and write.
단어를 바르게 배열하여 문장을 쓰세요.

_____
( email / she / Is / an / writing / ? )

## 16 Read and match.
알맞은 문장이 되도록 선으로 연결하세요.

(1) Where is •          • he doing?

(2) What is •          • he do?

(3) What does •          • he going?

## [17-18] Read and choose.
대화를 읽고 빈칸에 알맞은 것을 고르세요.

### 17
A: Is Dad cooking?
B: _____ He's sleeping.

ⓐ Yes, I am.          ⓑ No, she isn't.
ⓒ Yes, he is.          ⓓ No, he isn't.

### 18
A: _____
B: She's a police officer.

ⓐ Where is she?
ⓑ Where is she going?
ⓒ What does she do?
ⓓ What is she doing?

## [19-20] Look and write.
그림을 보고 대화의 빈칸에 알맞은 말을 쓰세요.

### 19

A: Where are you _____?
B: I'm going to the _____.

### 20

A: Can I have some _____, please?
B: Sure. _____ you are.

# Midterm TEST 3C

Institute

Name

Score /100

## [1-2] Listen and choose.
다음을 듣고 알맞은 그림을 고르세요.

**1** ⓐ  ⓑ

ⓒ 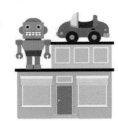 ⓓ

**2** ⓐ  ⓑ

ⓒ  ⓓ

## 3 Listen and choose.
다음을 듣고 그림에 알맞은 것을 고르세요.

ⓐ        ⓑ        ⓒ        ⓓ

## [4-5] Listen and mark O or X.
다음을 듣고 그림과 일치하면 ○ 표, 일치하지 않으면 X 표를 하세요.

**4**     **5**

(        )            (        )

## [6-7] Listen and choose.
다음을 듣고 그림에 알맞은 응답을 고르세요.

**6**

ⓐ        ⓑ        ⓒ        ⓓ

**7**

ⓐ        ⓑ        ⓒ        ⓓ

## 8 Listen and choose.
대화를 듣고 알맞은 그림을 고르세요.

ⓐ  ⓑ

ⓒ  ⓓ

## [9-10] Listen and choose.
다음을 듣고 알맞은 응답을 고르세요.

**9** ⓐ I'm hungry.

ⓑ No, thanks.

ⓒ Sure. Here you are.

ⓓ I'm going to the bakery.

**10** ⓐ He's crying.

ⓑ She's doing homework.

ⓒ He's a scientist.

ⓓ She's a dancer.

## 11 Read and choose.
다음을 읽고 알맞은 그림을 고르세요.

I drink milk every day.

ⓐ    ⓑ

ⓒ    ⓓ

## [12-13] Look and choose.
그림을 보고 알맞은 것을 고르세요.

### 12
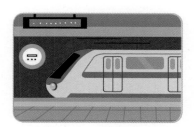

ⓐ Let's meet at the subway station.
ⓑ Let's meet at the bus stop.
ⓒ Let's meet at the gym.
ⓓ Let's meet at the playground.

### 13

ⓐ She likes sandwiches.
ⓑ She likes dumplings.
ⓒ She doesn't like fruit.
ⓓ She doesn't like spaghetti.

## 14 Look and write.
그림을 보고 빈칸에 알맞은 단어를 쓰세요.

   He wants _____.

## 15 Unscramble and write.
단어를 바르게 배열하여 문장을 쓰세요.

_____
( meet / at / Let's / the mall / . )

## 16 Read and choose.
알맞은 문장이 되도록 선으로 연결하세요.

(1) I drink •        • soda.

(2) I take •         • a diary.

(3) I write •        • a bath.

## [17-18] Read and choose.
대화를 읽고 빈칸에 알맞은 것을 고르세요.

### 17
A: What does she want?
B: _____

ⓐ I want a drone.
ⓑ We want in-line skates.
ⓒ He wants a game player.
ⓓ She wants a swim tube.

### 18
A: _____
B: Yes, he does. He likes vegetables.

ⓐ Does he like steak?
ⓑ Does he like hamburgers?
ⓒ Does he like onions?
ⓓ Does he like strawberries?

## [19-20] Look and write.
그림을 보고 대화의 빈칸에 알맞은 말을 쓰세요.

### 19

A: Do you _____ every day?
B: No, _____.

### 20

A: Let's meet at the _____.
   How about _____ _____ o'clock?
B: Okay. See you.

# Final TEST 3C

Institute _____

Name _____

Score _____ /100

## [1-2] Listen and choose.
다음을 듣고 알맞은 그림을 고르세요.

**1**
ⓐ
ⓑ
ⓒ
ⓓ

**2**
ⓐ
ⓑ
ⓒ
ⓓ

## 3 Listen and choose.
다음을 듣고 그림에 알맞은 것을 고르세요.

ⓐ    ⓑ    ⓒ    ⓓ

## [4-5] Listen and mark O or X.
대화를 듣고 그림과 일치하면 ○ 표, 일치하지 않으면 X 표를 하세요.

**4**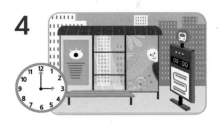
**5**

(     )          (     )

## 6 Listen and choose.
다음을 듣고 그림에 알맞은 응답을 고르세요.

ⓐ        ⓑ        ⓒ        ⓓ

## [7-8] Listen and choose.
대화를 듣고 알맞은 그림을 고르세요.

**7**
ⓐ
ⓑ
ⓒ
ⓓ

**8**
ⓐ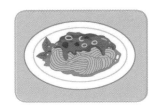
ⓑ
ⓒ
ⓓ

## [9-10] Listen and choose.
다음을 듣고 알맞은 응답을 고르세요.

**9**  ⓐ Yes, I am.          ⓑ No, I don't.
       ⓒ Sounds good.       ⓓ Sure. Here you are.

**10** ⓐ Yes, I do.          ⓑ No, thanks.
       ⓒ Okay. See you.      ⓓ It's seven o'clock.

# Let's Go · 3C

Unit  p. 5

Unit 4 p. 33

  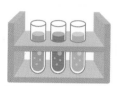 

Unit 6 p. 48

Unit 7 p. 61

# 2nd Edition

# LET'S GO

## to the English World

# 3c

# Word Book
# & Workbook

CHUNJAE EDUCATION, INC.

# Word Book

UNIT 1 ............ 2

UNIT 2 ............ 4

UNIT 3 ............ 6

UNIT 4 ............ 8

UNIT 5 ............ 10

UNIT 6 ............ 12

UNIT 7 ............ 14

UNIT 8 ............ 16

# Where Are You Going?

**A** Listen and repeat. 01 02

**park**
공원

**I'm going to the park.**
나는 공원에 가고 있어.

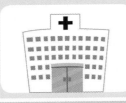

**hospital**
병원

**I'm going to the hospital.**
나는 병원에 가고 있어.

**bank**
은행

**I'm going to the bank.**
나는 은행에 가고 있어.

**bakery**
빵집

**I'm going to the bakery.**
나는 빵집에 가고 있어.

**toy shop**
장난감 가게

**He's going to the toy shop.**
그는 장난감 가게에 가고 있어.

**supermarket**
슈퍼마켓

**He's going to the supermarket.**
그는 슈퍼마켓에 가고 있어.

**bookstore**
서점

**She's going to the bookstore.**
그녀는 서점에 가고 있어.

**zoo**
동물원

**She's going to the zoo.**
그녀는 동물원에 가고 있어.

## B Read, write, and say.

**1  park**
공원

**2  hospital**
병원

**3  bank**
은행

**4  bakery**
빵집

**5  toy shop**
장난감 가게

**6  supermarket**
슈퍼마켓

**7  bookstore**
서점

**8  zoo**
동물원

### Learn More

| where | 어디에 | Where are you going? 너는 어디에 가고 있니? |
| to school | 학교에 | I'm going to school. 나는 학교에 가고 있어. |

**A** Listen and repeat. 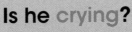 14 15

**crying**
울고 있는

**Is he crying?**
그는 울고 있니?

**doing homework**
숙제하고 있는

**Is she doing homework?**
그녀는 숙제하고 있니?

**playing tennis**
테니스를 치고 있는

**Is he playing tennis?**
그는 테니스를 치고 있니?

**playing games**
게임을 하고 있는

**Is she playing games?**
그녀는 게임을 하고 있니?

**riding a bike**
자전거를 타고 있는

**He's riding a bike.**
그는 자전거를 타고 있어.

**taking a shower**
샤워하고 있는

**She's taking a shower.**
그녀는 샤워하고 있어.

**driving**
운전하고 있는

**He's driving.**
그는 운전하고 있어.

**writing an email**
이메일을 쓰고 있는

**She's writing an email.**
그녀는 이메일을 쓰고 있어.

1 **crying**
울고 있는

2 **doing homework**
숙제하고 있는

3 **playing tennis**
테니스를 치고 있는

4 **playing games**
게임을 하고 있는

5 **riding a bike**
자전거를 타고 있는

6 **taking a shower**
샤워하고 있는

7 **driving**
운전하고 있는

8 **writing an email**
이메일을 쓰고 있는

## Learn More

**sleeping**
자고 있는

Is he sleeping? 그는 자고 있니?

**washing the dishes**
설거지를 하고 있는

Is she washing the dishes? 그녀는 설거지를 하고 있니?

**playing baseball**
야구를 하고 있는

Are they playing baseball? 그들은 야구를 하고 있니?

# Can I Have Some Water, Please?

## Ⓐ Listen and repeat. 🎧27 🎧28

**tea**
차

**Can I have some tea, please?**
차를 좀 마셔도 되나요?

**soup**
수프

**Can I have some soup, please?**
수프를 좀 먹어도 되나요?

**lemonade**
레모네이드

**Can I have some lemonade?**
레모네이드를 좀 마셔도 되니?

**iced water**
얼음물

**Can I have some iced water?**
얼음물을 좀 마셔도 되니?

**chips**
감자칩

**Do you want some chips?**
감자칩을 좀 먹을래?

**hot dogs**
핫도그

**Do you want some hot dogs?**
핫도그를 좀 먹을래?

**cereal**
시리얼

**Have some cereal.**
시리얼을 좀 먹어.

## B Read, write, and say.

☐ Read ☐ Write ☐ Say

**1 tea**
차

**2 soup**
수프

**3 lemonade**
레모네이드

**4 iced water**
얼음물

**5 chips**
감자칩

**6 hot dogs**
핫도그

**7 cereal**
시리얼

---

### Learn More

| | | |
|---|---|---|
| **thirsty** | 목마른 | I'm thirsty. 나는 목말라. |
| **hungry** | 배고픈 | I'm hungry. 나는 배고파. |
| **cold** | 추운 | I'm cold. 나는 추워. |

# UNIT 4 — What Does He Do?

**Ⓐ Listen and repeat.** 🎧40 🎧41

**scientist**
과학자

**She's a** scientist.
그녀는 과학자야.

**dancer**
댄서

**He's a** dancer.
그는 댄서야.

**vet**
수의사

**She's a** vet.
그녀는 수의사야.

**model**
모델

**She's a** model.
그녀는 모델이야.

**dentist**
치과 의사

**He's a** dentist.
그는 치과 의사야.

**soccer player**
축구 선수

**He's a** soccer player.
그는 축구 선수야.

**bus driver**
버스 운전사

**Is she a** bus driver?
그녀는 버스 운전사니?

**farmer**
농부

**Is he a** farmer?
그는 농부니?

## B Read, write, and say.

**1  scientist**
과학자

**2  dancer**
댄서

**3  vet**
수의사

**4  model**
모델

**5  dentist**
치과 의사

**6  soccer player**
축구 선수

**7  bus driver**
버스 운전사

**8  farmer**
농부

### Learn More

| | | |
|---|---|---|
| **cook** | 요리사 | I'm a cook. 나는 요리사야. |
| **singer** | 가수 | She's a singer. 그녀는 가수야. |
| **doctor** | 의사 | He's a doctor. 그는 의사야. |
| **police officer** | 경찰관 | Is she a police officer? 그녀는 경찰관이니? |
| **firefighter** | 소방관 | Is he a firefighter? 그는 소방관이니? |

# Do You Exercise Every Day?

**get up early**
일찍 일어나다

**Do you** get up early **every day?**
너는 매일 일찍 일어나니?

**eat breakfast**
아침을 먹다

**Do you** eat breakfast **every day?**
너는 매일 아침을 먹니?

**drink soda**
탄산음료를 마시다

**Do you** drink soda **every day?**
너는 매일 탄산음료를 마시니?

**clean your room**
네 방을 청소하다

**Do you** clean your room **every day?**
너는 매일 네 방을 청소하니?

**exercise**
운동하다

**I** exercise **every day.**
나는 매일 운동해.

**write a diary**
일기를 쓰다

**I** write a diary **every day.**
나는 매일 일기를 써.

**take a bath**
목욕하다

**I** take a bath **every day.**
나는 매일 목욕해.

## B Read, write, and say.

☐ Read  ☐ Write  ☐ Say

**1  get up early**
일찍 일어나다

**2  eat breakfast**
아침을 먹다

**3  drink soda**
탄산음료를 마시다

**4  clean your room**
네 방을 청소하다

**5  exercise**
운동하다

**6  write a diary**
일기를 쓰다

**7  take a bath**
목욕하다

---

### Learn More

**every day**  매일

**drink milk**  우유를 마시다

**That's not good.**  그것은 좋지 않아.

**Do you exercise** every day? 너는 매일 운동하니?

I drink milk **every day.** 나는 매일 우유를 마셔.

# He Wants a Skateboard

**A** **Listen and repeat.**  66  67

| | | |
|---|---|---|
|  | **a drone**<br>드론 | **He wants** a drone.<br>그는 드론을 원해. |
|  | **a skateboard**<br>스케이트보드 | **He wants** a skateboard.<br>그는 스케이트보드를 원해. |
|  | **a tennis racket**<br>테니스 라켓 | **She wants** a tennis racket.<br>그녀는 테니스 라켓을 원해. |
|  | **a swim tube**<br>수영 튜브 | **She wants** a swim tube.<br>그녀는 수영 튜브를 원해. |
|  | **a computer**<br>컴퓨터 | **I want** a computer.<br>나는 컴퓨터를 원해. |
|  | **a game player**<br>게임기 | **I want** a game player.<br>나는 게임기를 원해. |
|  | **in-line skates**<br>인라인스케이트화 | **Do you want** in-line skates?<br>너는 인라인스케이트화를 원하니? |
|  | **soccer shoes**<br>축구화 | **Do you want** soccer shoes?<br>너는 축구화를 원하니? |

## B Read, write, and say.

**1 a drone**
드론

**2 a skateboard**
스케이트보드

**3 a tennis racket**
테니스 라켓

**4 a swim tube**
수영 튜브

**5 a computer**
컴퓨터

**6 a game player**
게임기

**7 in-line skates**
인라인스케이트화

**8 soccer shoes**
축구화

### Learn More

| | | |
|---|---|---|
| **a beach ball** 비치 볼 | **Do you want** a beach ball? 너는 비치 볼을 원하니? |
| **a backpack** 배낭 | **He wants** a backpack. 그는 배낭을 원해. |
| **a hair band** 머리띠 | **She wants** a hair band. 그녀는 머리띠를 원해. |
| **It's mine.** 그것은 내 거야. | |

# Does She Like Salad?

**A** Listen and repeat.  79  80

**fruit**
과일

**Does he like fruit?**
그는 과일을 좋아하니?

**curry**
카레

**Does he like curry?**
그는 카레를 좋아하니?

**steak**
스테이크

**Does she like steak?**
그녀는 스테이크를 좋아하니?

**spaghetti**
스파게티

**Does she like spaghetti?**
그녀는 스파게티를 좋아하니?

**vegetables**
채소

**He likes vegetables.**
그는 채소를 좋아해.

**sandwiches**
샌드위치

**She likes sandwiches.**
그녀는 샌드위치를 좋아해.

**hamburgers**
햄버거

**He doesn't like hamburgers.**
그는 햄버거를 좋아하지 않아.

**dumplings**
만두

**She doesn't like dumplings.**
그녀는 만두를 좋아하지 않아.

## B Read, write, and say.

**1 fruit**
과일

**2 curry**
카레

**3 steak**
스테이크

**4 spaghetti**
스파게티

**5 vegetables**
채소

**6 sandwiches**
샌드위치

**7 hamburgers**
햄버거

**8 dumplings**
만두

### Learn More

| | | |
|---|---|---|
| **like** | 좋아하다 | I like fruit. 나는 과일을 좋아해. |
| **salad** | 샐러드 | Does she like salad? 그녀는 샐러드를 좋아하니? |
| **chicken** | 치킨 | Does he like chicken? 그는 치킨을 좋아하니? |
| **fish** | 생선 | Jenny likes fish. 제니는 생선을 좋아해. |

# Let's Meet at the Park

**A** **Listen and repeat.**  92  93

**mall**
쇼핑몰

Let's meet at the mall.
쇼핑몰에서 만나자.

**playground**
놀이터

Let's meet at the playground.
놀이터에서 만나자.

**library**
도서관

Let's meet at the library.
도서관에서 만나자.

**museum**
박물관

Let's go to the museum.
박물관에 가자.

**bus stop**
버스 정류장

Let's meet at the bus stop at 6.
버스 정류장에서 6시에 만나자.

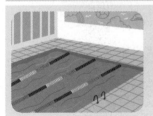

**swimming pool**
수영장

Let's go to the swimming pool.
수영장에 가자.

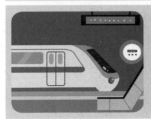

**subway station**
지하철역

Let's meet at the subway station at 4.
지하철역에서 4시에 만나자.

## B Read, write, and say.

**1 mall**
쇼핑몰

**2 playground**
놀이터

**3 library**
도서관

**4 museum**
박물관

**5 bus stop**
버스 정류장

**6 swimming pool**
수영장

**7 subway station**
지하철역

### Learn More

| | | |
|---|---|---|
| **How about ...?** ~이 어때? | How about **at one o'clock?** 1시가 어때? |
| **at+장소** ~에서 | Let's meet **at the mall.** 쇼핑몰에서 만나자. |
| **at+시각** ~(시)에 | Let's meet **at two o'clock.** 2시에 만나자. |

# Workbook 3c

UNIT **1** · · · · · · · · · · · · 20      UNIT **5** · · · · · · · · · · · · 44

UNIT **2** · · · · · · · · · · · · 26      UNIT **6** · · · · · · · · · · · · 50

UNIT **3** · · · · · · · · · · · · 32      UNIT **7** · · · · · · · · · · · · 56

UNIT **4** · · · · · · · · · · · · 38      UNIT **8** · · · · · · · · · · · · 62

# Where Are You Going?

## Words

### A Look and check.

1
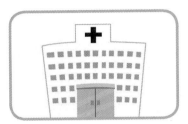
- [ ] toy shop
- [ ] hospital

2

- [ ] park
- [ ] bank

3

- [ ] park
- [ ] bakery

4

- [ ] bookstore
- [ ] supermarket

5

- [ ] zoo
- [ ] bakery

6

- [ ] hospital
- [ ] supermarket

7

- [ ] zoo
- [ ] bank

8

- [ ] toy shop
- [ ] bookstore

# Practice

## A Read and circle T or F.

**1**

T
F

I'm going to the supermarket.

**2**
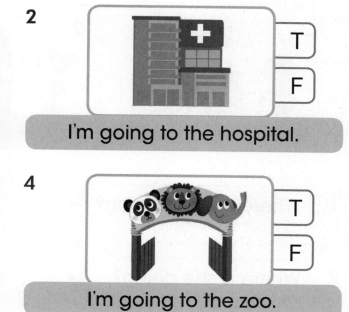
T
F

I'm going to the hospital.

**3**

T
F

I'm going to the bakery.

**4**
T
F

I'm going to the zoo.

## B Follow, choose, and write.

bank    bookstore    toy shop

**1**
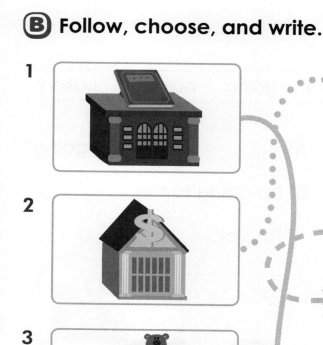

A: Where are you going?

B: I'm going to the _____.

**2**

A: Where are you going?

B: I'm going to the _____.

**3**
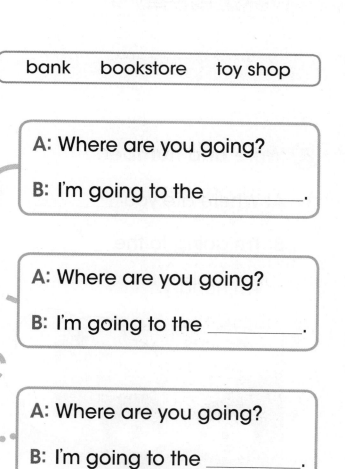

A: Where are you going?

B: I'm going to the _____.

# Listen & Talk

## (A) Look, match, and write.

| bank | toy shop | supermarket |

1  | Where are you going? | •    • | She's going to the _____ .

2  | Where is she going? | •    • | I'm going to the _____ .

3  | Where is he going? | •    • | He's going to the _____ .

| Where | going | hospital | bakery |

## (B) Write and number.

1  A: Where are you _____ ?

    B: I'm going to the _____ .

    I'm hungry.

2  A: _____ are you going?

    B: I'm going to the _____ .

    I'm sick.

# Write & Talk

## Ⓐ Look and write.

**1**

A: _____ are you going?

B: I'm _____ to the toy shop.

**2**

A: Where is she _____?

B: She's going to the _____.

**3**

A: Where is _____ going?

B: He's going to the _____.

He's sick.

A: That's too _____.

**4**

A: Where are _____ going?

B: I'm going to the _____. I'm hungry.

**5**

A: Hi, Jack. _____ are you?

B: I'm great.

A: Where are you going?

B: I'm going _____ the _____.

# Story

## A Write and number in order.

Where _____ we going?

I don't know.

_____ are you going?

I'm going to the _____.

We're _____ to the zoo.

We're going to the _____.

## B Choose and write.

1

A: Where are you going?

B: _____

A: Let's go together.

B: Okay.

2

A: _____

B: I'm going to the hospital.

I'm sick.

A: That's too bad.

# Writing

## Ⓐ Make the sentence.

**1**

are | ? | you | Where | going

····▸ _____

너는 어디에 가고 있니?

**2**

the | . | going | bookstore | I'm | to

····▸ _____

나는 서점에 가고 있어.

**3**

going | Where | he | is | ?

····▸ _____

그는 어디에 가고 있니?

**4**

to | He's | bank | going | . | the

····▸ _____

그는 은행에 가고 있어.

**5**

going | park | the | . | to | She's

····▸ _____

그녀는 공원에 가고 있어.

# Words

**A** Choose and write.

1

_____

2

_____

3

_____

4

_____

doing homework

playing games

driving

writing an email

riding a bike

crying

playing tennis

taking a shower

5

_____

6

_____

7

_____

8

_____

# Practice

## Ⓐ Read and write the letter.

**1** Is he doing homework? ☐

**2** Is she riding a bike? ☐

**3** Is she crying? ☐

**4** Is he taking a shower? ☐

## Ⓑ Circle and write.

**1**

A: Is she _____?

( crying / driving )

B: Yes, she is.

**2**

A: Is he _____?

( writing an email / playing games )

B: Yes, he is.

**3**

A: Is she riding a bike?

B: _____

( Yes, she is. / No, she isn't. )

# Listen & Talk

## A Read and match.

1      2     3

1 | Is he crying? | •      • | Yes, she is. |

2 | Is she taking a shower? | •      • | Yes, he is. |

3 | Is he doing homework? | •      • | No, he isn't. He's writing an email. |

## B Look and write.

> driving
> playing games
> playing tennis

1

A: Are you _____?

B: Yes, _____.

2

A: Is she playing soccer?

B: No, _____.

    She's _____.

3

A: Is he _____?

B: Yes, _____.

# Write & Talk

**Ⓐ Look and write.**

1

**A:** Is she _____?

**B:** _____, she is.

2

**A:** Is John _____?

**B:** Yes, he _____.

3

**A:** Are you _____ a shower?

**B:** No, I'm _____.

    I'm _____.

4

**A:** Is Tony _____?

**B:** No, _____.

**A:** What is he _____?

**B:** He's _____.

5

**A:** _____ you cooking?

**B:** No, _____.

    I'm _____.

# Story

## A Read and write T or F.

**1**

A: Is he sleeping?

B: No, he isn't. He's driving.

**2**

A: Is she playing baseball?

B: Yes, she is.

**3**

A: Are you crying?

B: Yes, I am.

## B Choose and write.

| Yes, he is. | He's taking a shower. |
| No, he isn't. | Is he doing homework? |

**1**

A: John is in the bedroom.

B: _____

A: Yes, he is.

**2**

A: Is Mike playing games?

B: _____

A: What is he doing?

B: _____

# Writing

## A Make the sentence.

**1**

| she | ? | doing | Is | homework |

····▶ _____

그녀는 숙제를 하고 있니?

**2**

| He's | a | riding | . | bike |

····▶ _____

그는 자전거를 타고 있어.

**3**

| she | an | Is | ? | writing | email |

····▶ _____

그녀는 이메일을 쓰고 있니?

**4**

| playing | She's | . | games |

····▶ _____

그녀는 게임을 하고 있어.

**5**

| ? | shower | Are | taking | you | a |

····▶ _____

너는 샤워를 하고 있니?

# Can I Have Some Water, Please?

# Words

**A** Read and match.

1  chips    2  cereal    3  soup    4  tea

a
b
c
d

e
f
g

5  iced water    6  lemonade    7  hot dogs

# Practice

## (A) Look and circle.

**1**

I'm ( hungry / thirsty ).

Can I have some ( iced water / hot dogs ), please?

**2**

I'm ( hungry / thirsty ).

Can I have some ( soup / cereal ), please?

## (B) Choose and write.

| cold | thirsty | hungry |
|------|---------|--------|
| tea | hot dogs | lemonade |

**1**

A: I'm _____.

Can I have some _____, please?

B: Sure. Here you are.

**2**

A: I'm _____.

Can I have some _____, please?

B: Sure. Here you are.

**3**

A: I'm _____.

Can I have some _____, please?

B: Sure. Here you are.

# Listen & Talk

**A** **Read and write the letter.**

**1**
> **A:** I'm cold. Can I have some soup, please?
> **B:** Sure. Here you are.

**2**
> **A:** I'm hungry. Can I have some cereal, please?
> **B:** Sure. Here you are.

**3**
> **A:** I'm thirsty. Can I have some juice, please?
> **B:** Sure. Here you are.

**B** **Choose and write.**

**1**

**A:** I'm _____. Can I have

some _____, please?

**B:** Sure. Here you are.

**2**

**A:** I'm _____. Can I have

some _____, please?

**B:** Sure. Here you are.

| thirsty | cold | hungry | iced water | tea | chips |

# Write & Talk

## A Look and write.

**1**

A: I'm _____.

Can I have some _____, please?

B: Sure. Here you are.

**2**

A: I'm _____.

Can I have some _____, please?

B: Sure. _____ you are.

A: Thank you.

**3**

A: I'm _____.

Can I have some _____, please?

B: Sure. Here _____ are.

**4**

A: Do you _____ _____ orange juice?

B: No, thanks.

Can I _____ some _____, please?

A: Sure.

**5**

A: I'm hungry.

_____ _____ have some pizza?

B: Sure. Have some _____, too.

# Story

## (A) Read and write the letter.

**1**

> Sure.

- (a) Have some lemonade.
- (b) Sure. Here you are.
- (c) Can I have some hot dogs, please?

**2**

**3**

> Can I have some ice cream, please?

## (B) Follow and write.

**1**

A: I'm _____. Can I have some _____, please?

B: Sure. Here you are.

**2**

A: I'm _____. Can I have some _____, please?

B: Sure. Here you are.

**3**

A: I'm _____. Can I have some _____, please?

B: Sure. Here you are.

# Writing

## Ⓐ Make the sentence.

**1**

thirsty   .   I'm

····▶ _____

나는 목이 말라.

**2**

have   I   Can   some   hamburgers   ?

····▶ _____

햄버거를 좀 먹어도 될까?

**3**

I   Can   have   please   some   cereal,   ?

····▶ _____

시리얼을 좀 먹어도 될까?

**4**

soup   Do   want   you   some   ?

····▶ _____

수프를 좀 먹을래?

**5**

ice cream   Have   .   some

····▶ _____

아이스크림을 좀 먹어.

# What Does He Do?

## Words

**A** Match and write.

1

_____

bus driver

dancer

5

_____

2

_____

scientist

model

6

_____

3

_____

soccer player

dentist

7

_____

4

_____

farmer

vet

8

_____

# Practice

## (A) Read and choose.

**1** | She's a bus driver.

 **a**     **b**

**2** | He's a model.

 **a**     **b**

**3** | He's a scientist.

 **a**     **b**

**4** | She's a dentist.

 **a**     **b**

## (B) Circle and write.

**1**

A: What does he do?

B: He's a _____.
    ( dentist / soccer player )

**2**

A: What does she do?

B: She's a _____.
    ( dancer / farmer )

**3**

A: What does he do?

B: He's a _____.
    ( bus driver / vet )

# Listen & Talk

## (A) Read and circle.

**1**

A: What does ( he / she ) do?

B: She's a ( vet / dentist ).

**2**

A: What does ( he / she ) do?

B: He's a ( scientist / bus driver ).

**3**

A: What does ( he / she ) do?

B: She's a ( farmer / dancer ).

vet
scientist
soccer player

## (B) Follow and write.

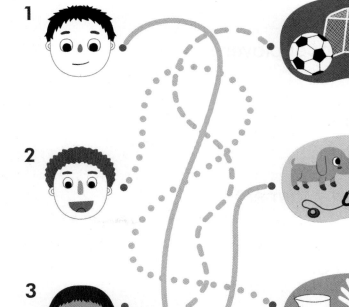

**1**

A: _____ does she do?

B: She's a _____.

**2**

A: What does _____ do?

B: He's a _____.

**3**

A: What does he _____?

B: He's a _____.

40

# Write & Talk

## Ⓐ Make the sentence.

**1**

A: _____ does she do?

B: She's a _____.

**2**

A: What does he _____?

B: He's a _____.

**3**

A: Is he a model?

B: No, he _____.

　　He's a _____.

**4**

A: _____ is he?

B: He's my uncle.

A: What _____ _____ do?

B: He's a _____.

**5**

A: That's my mom.

B: What _____ _____ do?

A: She's a _____.

# Story

## A Read and circle T or F.

**1**  She's a police officer.
She's tall.    T  F

**2**  They're not dancers.
They're cooks.    T  F

**3**  He's a singer.    T  F

## B Read, match, and write.

**1**     **2**     **3**     **4**

**1** What does she do?    •    •    No, she isn't. She's a _____.

**2** What does he do?    •    •    She's a _____.

**3** Is she a bus driver?    •    •    No, he isn't. He's a _____.

**4** Is he a dentist?    •    •    He's a _____.

# Writing

**A** Make the sentence.

1

does | do | he | What | ?

····▶ _____

그는 무슨 일을 하니?

2

a | He's | . | scientist

····▶ _____

그는 과학자야.

3

? | What | she | do | does

····▶ _____

그녀는 무슨 일을 하니?

4

dancer | a | She's | .

····▶ _____

그녀는 댄서야.

5

he | ? | a | Is | dentist

····▶ _____

그는 치과 의사니?

# Do You Exercise Every Day?

# Words

**A** Choose and write.

1

_____

2

_____

3

_____

4

_____

5

_____

6

_____

7

_____

| | |
|---|---|
| drink soda | get up early |
| exercise | write a diary |
| take a bath | eat breakfast |
| clean your room | |

# Practice

## Ⓐ Read and check.

**1**

☐ I clean my room every day.

☐ I get up early every day.

**2**

☐ I take a bath every day.

☐ I drink soda every day.

## Ⓑ Follow, write, and circle.

**1** O

A: Do you _____ every day?

B: ( Yes, I do. / No, I don't. )

**2** O

A: Do you _____ every day?

B: ( Yes, I do. / No, I don't. )

**3** X

A: Do you _____ every day?

B: ( Yes, I do. / No, I don't. )

| write a diary | exercise | eat breakfast |

# Listen & Talk

## (A) Read and number.

1  A: Do you write a diary every day?
   B: Yes, I do.

2  A: Do you get up early every day?
   B: No, I don't.

3  A: Do you take a bath every day?
   B: Yes, I do.

4  A: Do you clean your room every day?
   B: No, I don't.

## (B) Write and match.

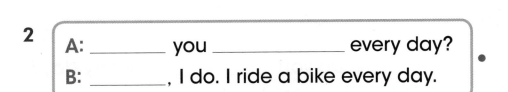

eat breakfast    exercise    drink soda

1  A: Do you _____ every day?
   B: _____, I do. I eat bread for breakfast.

2  A: _____ you _____ every day?
   B: _____, I do. I ride a bike every day.

3  A: _____ you _____ every day?
   B: _____, I don't. I drink milk every day.

# Write & Talk

**Ⓐ Look and write.**

**1**

A: Do you _____ every day?

B: _____, I do.

**2**

A: Do you _____ every day?

B: No, I _____.

**3**

A: _____ you _____ every day?

B: _____, I don't.

**4**

A: What's this?

B: It's my diary.

A: _____ you _____ every day?

B: Yes, I _____.

**5**

A: Do you like soda?

B: Yes, I do. I _____ every day.

A: That's _____ good.

# Story

## Ⓐ Read and write the letter.

**1**

Yes, I do.

> ⓐ Yes, I do.
> ⓑ No, I don't.
> ⓒ Do you watch TV every day?
> ⓓ Do you drink soda every day?

**2**

Yes, I do.

**3**

Do you exercise every day?

## Ⓑ Look and write.

**1**

A: Do you _____ every day?

B: _____, I _____.

**2**

A: _____ you _____ every day?

B: Yes, _____.

**3**

A: Do you _____ every day?

B: _____, _____.

# Writing

## Ⓐ Make the sentence.

**1**

| every day | I | . | write | a diary |

···▶ _____

나는 매일 일기를 써.

**2**

| I | early | every day | get up | . |

···▶ _____

나는 매일 일찍 일어나.

**3**

| Do | exercise | you | every day | ? |

···▶ _____

너는 매일 운동하니?

**4**

| ? | you | every day | Do | eat breakfast |

···▶ _____

너는 매일 아침을 먹니?

**5**

| soda | drink | you | Do | ? | every day |

···▶ _____

너는 매일 탄산음료를 마시니?

# He Wants a Skateboard

## Words

**(A)** Follow, choose, and write.

a drone        a computer
a skateboard   a game player
a swim tube    a tennis racket
in-line skates soccer shoes

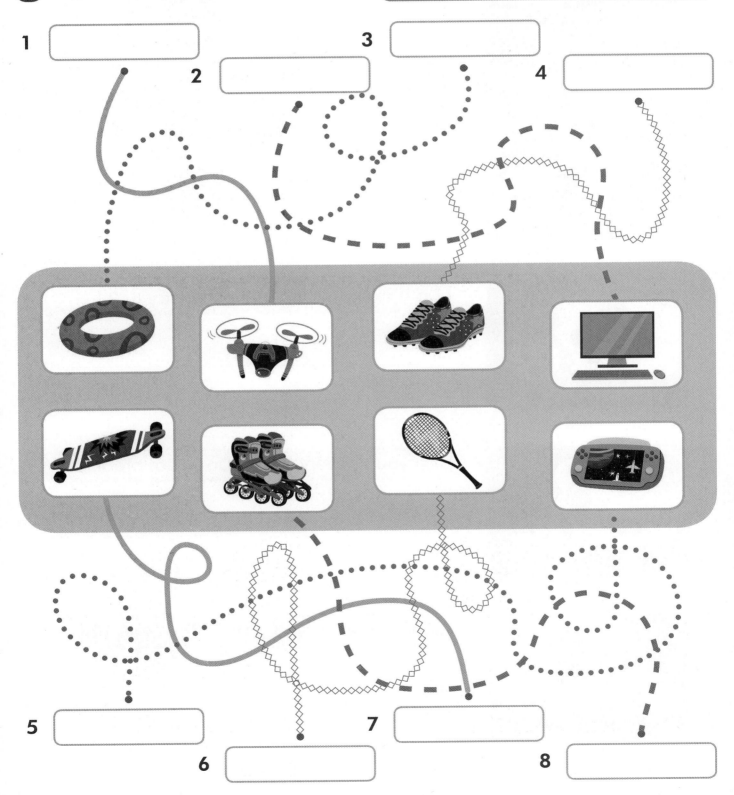

1 [ ]

2 [ ]

3 [ ]

4 [ ]

5 [ ]

6 [ ]

7 [ ]

8 [ ]

# Practice

## A Read and check.

**1**

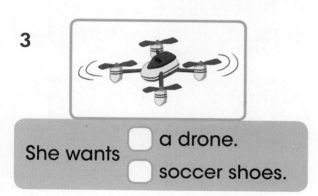

He wants ☐ a game player.
☐ a computer.

**2**

She wants ☐ in-line skates.
☐ a skateboard.

**3**

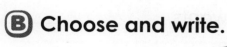

She wants ☐ a drone.
☐ soccer shoes.

**4**

He wants ☐ a tennis racket.
☐ a swim tube.

## B Choose and write.

| a swim tube | soccer shoes |
| a game player | a skateboard |

**1**

A: What does he want?

B: He wants _____.

**2**

A: What does she want?

B: She wants _____.

# Listen & Talk

## Ⓐ Read and write the letter.

**1**
A: What does he want?
B: He wants soccer shoes. ☐

**2**
A: What does he want?
B: He wants in-line skates. ☐

**3**
A: What does she want?
B: She wants a game player. ☐

**4**
A: What does she want?
B: She wants a computer. ☐

## Ⓑ Follow and write.

| a tennis racket | a swim tube | a skateboard |

**1**

A: _____ does she want?

B: She wants _____.

**2**

A: What does he _____?

B: He wants _____.

**3**

A: What _____ she want?

B: She wants _____.

# Write & Talk

**(A) Look and write.**

1

A: _____ do you want?

B: I want _____.

2

A: What does she _____ for Christmas?

B: She wants _____.

3

A: What _____ he want?

B: He _____ _____.

4

A: Anna _____ want a swim tube.

B: What does she _____?

A: She _____ _____.

5

A: Do you want a tennis racket?

B: No, _____.

A: _____ do you want?

B: I _____ _____.

# Story

## (A) Read and write the answer.

**1**

| Does Jane want a drone? |

····▸ _____

**2**

| Does Jack want a skateboard? |

····▸ _____

**3**

| Does Emily want a swim tube? |

····▸ No, she doesn't. She _____.

## (B) Look and write.

**1**

A: Kate doesn't want a skateboard.

B: What _____ want?

A: She _____.

**2**

A: _____ Ted want in-line skates?

B: No, he _____.

He _____.

54

# Writing

## Ⓐ Make the sentence.

**1**

| does | want | What | ? | she |

····▸ _____

그녀는 무엇을 원하니?

**2**

| wants | . | She | a skateboard |

····▸ _____

그녀는 스케이트보드를 원해.

**3**

| a game player | you | Do | want | ? |

····▸ _____

너는 게임기를 원하니?

**4**

| . | a swim tube | wants | He |

····▸ _____

그는 수영 튜브를 원해.

**5**

| a drone | He | want | doesn't | . |

····▸ _____

그는 드론을 원하지 않아.

# Does She Like Salad?

## Words

**A** Find, circle, and match.

1

2

3

v e g f r u i t c u v e g e t a b l e s f r s t e a k b u

4

5

6

s c u r r y o s a n d w i c h e s c u s p a g h e t t i e

7

8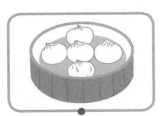

f e n h a m b u r g e r s b a d u m p l i n g s h u

# Practice

## A Read and choose.

**1** He likes spaghetti.

a b

**2** She likes hamburgers.

a b

**3** He doesn't like curry.

a b

**4** She doesn't like dumplings.

a b

## B Look and write.

steak

sandwiches

fruit

vegetables

**1** A: Does she like _____?

B: Yes, she does.

**2** A: Does he like _____?

B: Yes, he does.

**3** A: Does he like _____?

B: No, he doesn't.

**4** A: Does she like _____?

B: No, she doesn't.

# Listen & Talk

## A Read and write T or F.

**1**
A: Does she like steak?
B: Yes, she does.

**2**
A: Does he like dumplings?
B: Yes, he does.

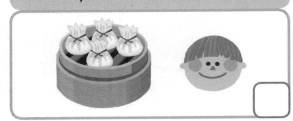

**3**
A: What does he like?
B: He likes vegetables.

**4**
A: What does she like?
B: She likes fruit.

## B Read and write.

| curry | hamburgers | Yes | Does |
|-------|-----------|-----|------|
| fruit | sandwiches | No | doesn't |

**1**

A: _____ he like _____?

B: _____, he does.

**2**

A: Does she like _____?

B: No, she _____.

**3**

A: Does he like _____?

B: _____, he doesn't. He likes _____.

58

# Write & Talk

**Ⓐ Look and write.**

**1**

A: Does she like _____?

B: Yes, she _____.

**2**

A: _____ he like _____?

B: No, he doesn't.

He likes _____.

**3**

A: Does he like grapes?

B: No, he _____.

He _____ _____ fruit.

**4**

A: Does Kelly like _____?

B: No, _____ doesn't.

A: _____ _____ she like?

B: She likes _____.

**5**

A: I'm making spaghetti. It's for my dad.

B: Does your dad like _____?

A: Yes, _____.

# Story

## A Read and write the answer.

**1**

Does she like milk?

···▶ _____

**2**

Does she like fruit?

···▶ _____

**3**

Does she like apples?

···▶ _____

## B Follow and write.

**1**

A: What does she _____?

B: She likes _____.

**2**

A: Does he like _____?

B: Yes, he _____.

**3**

A: Does she like _____?

B: No, she _____.

# Writing

## Ⓐ Make the sentence.

**1**

like  ?  Does  hamburgers  she

····▸ _____

그녀는 햄버거를 좋아하니?

**2**

he  vegetables  like  ?  Does

····▸ _____

그는 채소를 좋아하니?

**3**

.  likes  She  fruit

····▸ _____

그녀는 과일을 좋아해.

**4**

spaghetti  doesn't  .  He  like

····▸ _____

그는 스파게티를 좋아하지 않아.

**5**

doesn't  She  steak  .  like

····▸ _____

그녀는 스테이크를 좋아하지 않아.

# Let's Meet at the Park

# Words

**A** Circle and write.

1

playground | bakery

_____

2
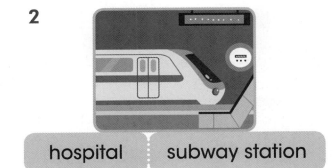
hospital | subway station

_____

3
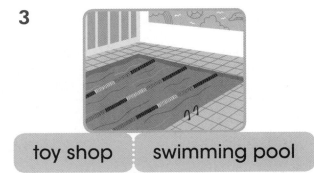
toy shop | swimming pool

_____

4

bus stop | bookstore

_____

5

bank | museum

_____

6

mall | park

_____

7

zoo | library

_____

# Practice

## A Look and circle.

**1**

Let's meet at the ( bus stop / playground ).

How about at ( one o'clock / eleven o'clock )?

**2**

Let's meet at the ( swimming pool / subway station ).

How about at ( four thirty / two twenty )?

**3**

Let's meet at the ( library / museum ).

How about at ( twelve ten / ten twelve )?

| bus stop | mall | library |
|----------|------|---------|
| seven fifty | five thirty | nine forty |

## B Follow and write.

**1**

A: Let's meet at the _____.

How about at _____?

B: Okay. See you.

**2**

A: Let's meet at the _____.

How about at _____?

B: Okay. See you.

**3**

A: Let's meet at the _____.

How about at _____?

B: Okay. See you.

# Listen & Talk

## Ⓐ Match and write the time.

**1**

A: Let's meet at the library.
How about at one o'clock?

B: Okay.

**2**

A: Let's meet at the museum.
How about at three thirty?

B: Okay. See you.

**3**

A: Let's meet at the bus stop.
How about at five fifteen?

B: Okay. See you.

## Ⓑ Read and write.

| swimming pool | subway station | gym |
|---|---|---|

**1**

A: Let's meet at the _____.

How about at _____?

B: Okay. See you.

**2**

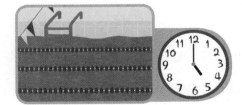

A: Let's go to the _____.

Let's meet at _____.

B: Okay. See you.

**3**

A: Let's meet at the _____.

How about at _____?

B: Okay. See you.

# Write & Talk

## (A) Look and write.

**1**

A: Let's exercise together.

B: _____ good.

A: _____ meet at the _____.

**2**

A: Let's read books.

B: Okay. Let's meet _____ the library _____ nine o'clock.

**3**

A: Let's meet at the _____ at three o'clock.

B: Sorry. I'm busy in the afternoon.

A: How about at _____?

B: Okay.

**4**

A: Let's meet at the _____.

_____ _____ at two fifteen?

B: Okay. See you.

**5**

A: Let's go to the _____.

B: Sounds _____.

A: Let's meet at one thirty.

B: Okay. _____ you.

# Story

## Ⓐ Read and write the letter.

**1** Sorry, I can't. How about Sunday?

ⓐ How about at 11 o'clock?
ⓑ Let's go to the museum today.
ⓒ Let's meet at the subway station.

**2** Okay.

**3** Okay. See you.

## Ⓑ Look and write.

**1**

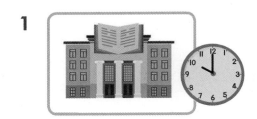

A: _____ meet at the _____.

How about at _____ o'clock?

B: Okay.

**2**

A: Let's _____ at the _____.

How _____ at _____?

B: Okay. _____ you.

**3**

A: Let's meet _____ the _____.

How about _____?

B: Okay. See you.

# Writing

## A Make the sentence.

**1**

| the swimming pool | go | Let's | . | to |

···▸ _____

수영장에 가자.

**2**

| at | How | three | about | ? | o'clock |

···▸ _____

3시가 어때?

**3**

| about | ? | at | How | four | thirty |

···▸ _____

4시 30분이 어때?

**4**

| at | meet | . | the bus stop | Let's |

···▸ _____

버스 정류장에서 만나자.

**5**

| at two o'clock. | Let's meet | at the gym |

···▸ _____

체육관에서 2시에 만나자.